TO ABBY, NOAH AND HADLEY,
BEST WISHES!

Colonel
Washington
and Me

Colonel Washington and Me

Siegle Books

Library of Congress Control Number: 2011962942
ISBN 978-0-9852819-0-8 (Hardbound) $16.95
ISBN 978-0-9852819-1-5 (Softbound) $11.95

Printed in the USA

www.colonelwashingtonandme.com

*This book is dedicated to my wife Kimberly and
my two sons, Jeffrey E. Jr and Peter J. Finegan*

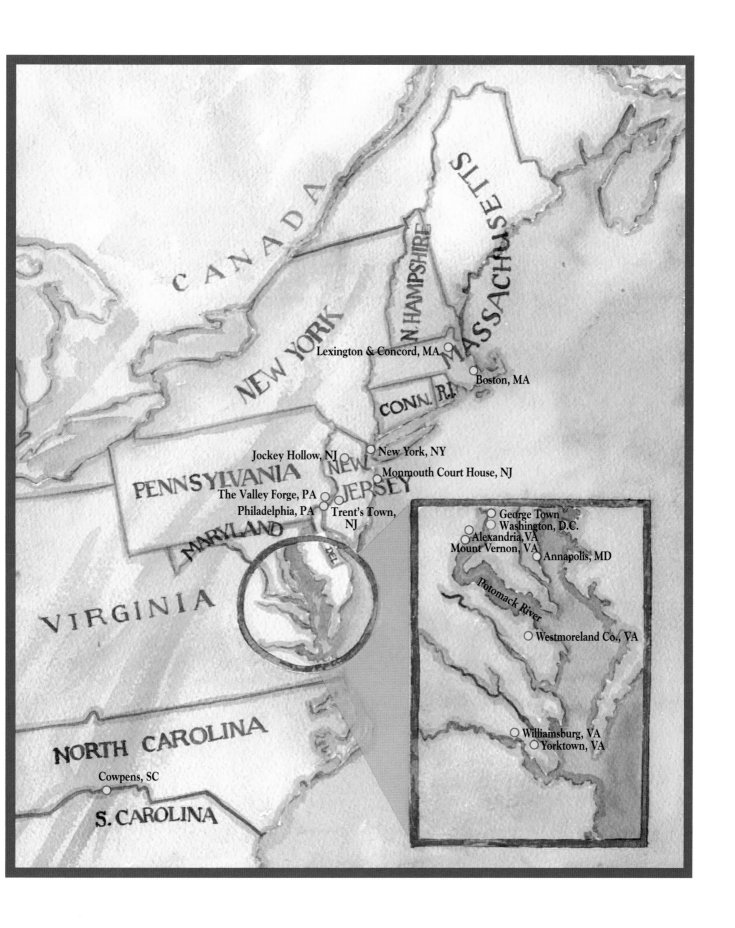

Acknowledgments

Introducing the young reader to the sensitive topic of slavery and the father of our country, while striking the proper tone of our main character, was more of a task than originally thought.

~

While many people assisted in numerous ways there are several who need to be mentioned specifically. Maryann McFadden was a wonderful resource for all questions relating to the publishing of this book. If she did not know the answer she assisted in finding it. Without Joseph Rubinfine the dream of collecting Washington manuscripts would have never become a reality.

~

My editor, Stephanie Nikolopoulos, was unbelievably helpful in pulling the story together and keeping my thought process on track. Her expertise in the editing of children's stories and her enthusiasm for developing the character of William Lee went way beyond my expectations.

~

Equally as helpful, but from a historic perspective was Mary V. Thompson, research historian at Mount Vernon. To have the expert on the enslaved community at Mount Vernon assisting with research was beyond my wildest dreams. Mary was then gracious enough to review the manuscript and edit it for historic accuracy while making suggestions and comments that enhanced the story.

~

The book did not truly come to life until I entered the shop of Preston Hindmarch. I presented the idea for the book to Preston and he embraced it with incredible enthusiasm. His artwork speaks for itself. In addition to his art, he took on the role of project manager all the way to laying out the final form that you see on these pages. To him I owe an enormous debt of gratitude!

~

Jeffrey E. Finegan Sr.
December, 2011

Colonel
Washington
and Me

George Washington, His Slave William Lee and Their Incredible Journey Together.
It's a story of freedom!

Written by Jeffrey E. Finegan Sr. ~ Illustrated by Preston Keith Hindmarch

Will, now up in years, meets with children living on the estate in the Mount Vernon kitchen. They have asked him to share his story of his life with General Washington.

Chapter I

My life with George Washington? It would be a pleasure to tell you the story. Well, he was called Colonel Washington when I first joined the family. Looking back on all those years I would never have guessed that the man who became my new master would lead me on such an interesting journey through history. I'm glad you joined me in the kitchen here at Mount Vernon. It's a cozy spot, so warm up next to the fire and join me as we travel back in time!

I was born into slavery around 1752. The law in British Colonial America allowed another person to own me just because I was of African descent. I was the property of the Lee family of Westmoreland County, Virginia, and, by law, they had the right to sell me whenever they wanted. I could be separated from my family at a moment's notice, never to return. I had the same heart and mind as any other person; how could

Along with his brother Frank, Will arrives at Mount Vernon, George Washington's estate on the Potomac River. No doubt nervous about his new home and master, Will could have never imagined that he would be part of the great historic events that lay ahead.

they consider me property? Nevertheless, in 1768 the Lee family sold me to Colonel Washington for 61 pounds and 15 shillings, the British currency used by the colonials at the time. I was only about sixteen years old when I was separated from my family, and I continued to use the Lee name throughout my life. Luckily for me, the Washingtons purchased my brother Frank at the same time so I was not completely alone in my new home. My brother and I were filled with anxiety as we traveled north. We had no idea who our new master was or what sort of person he would turn out to be.

Washington was, by far, the tallest man I had ever laid eyes on. He stood almost six feet and three inches and was dressed impeccably. Colonel and Mrs. Washington lived at Mount Vernon, a plantation overlooking the Potomack River, near Alexandria, Virginia. Back then Washington's mansion was not nearly as large as it is now, but it was still beautiful. George Washington had a great eye for luxurious fabric and selected most, if not all, of the furnishings and decorations in the home.

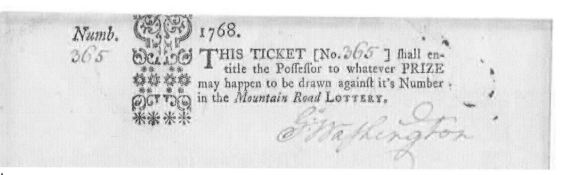

Upon our arrival we went directly to work in the mansion, instead of the field, so I evidently stood out in the colonel's eye. Those of us who worked in the home wore beautiful uniforms and expensive shoes with buckles that allowed us to stand out from all the other slaves who labored in the field. Although I enjoyed wearing the bright colors Colonel Washington selected for us I had mixed feelings. When I observed that the colonel's field slaves were issued only a few shirts and pairs of pants for the entire year, it filled me with remorse.

Being slaves always cast a shadow on life, but we made the best of it. We were always under the watchful and demanding eye of Colonel and Mrs. Washington. As house servants, we found ourselves at the center of plantation life. This had some advantages, like the occasional extra biscuit or slice of ham that somehow found their way to us.

Washington was a very capable man. When he was younger he worked as a surveyor, before serving honorably in the French and Indian War. It was in this war that he earned the rank of colonel for his leadership and bravery. The French and Indian War was fought between the British and the French, with various Native American Indian tribes fighting for both sides. Although the war did not officially end until 1763, Colonel Washington retired his Virginian colonelcy in 1758. Waiting for his hand in marriage was the lovely young widow Martha Dandridge Custis. They wed in January 1759 and along with the two young children from her previous marriage they made their way to their new home on the Potomack. With the war behind him,

Hand drawn and signed survey executed by an eighteen-year-old George Washington in 1750.

Colonel
Washington
and Me

Washington entered the world of politics. He was elected as a member of the House of Burgesses, where he and his neighbors helped govern the colony of Virginia. Washington was the third generation of his family born in the colonies and, like those who came before him, remained a proud British subject. He was born into a society where owning another person was commonplace. I found out after I was here for a

Will had to perfect his riding skills when fox hunting with George Washington. His equestrian abilities were helpful later in the Revolutionary War.

while that he became a slaveholder when he was only eleven years old! That is how old he was when his father died, leaving young George "property" in his will. Property in this case meant not only land but people too.

Not long after my arrival, Colonel Washington informed me that I would serve in the capacity of valet de chamber, in other words, his personal servant. That meant that I started and ended my day with the colonel and very rarely left his side. Our days were long. Washington rose before the sun came up, and the day did not end until I had helped him accomplish many tasks. The colonel was

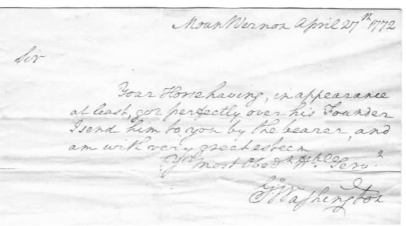

Written by George Washington in 1772 to his good friend James Tilghman in Alexandria, this letter was most likely hand delivered by William Lee.

still an active surveyor, and I accompanied him on his trips to the frontier. He had the best eye for good fertile land of anyone I knew, and he eventually owned thousands of

Colonel Washington and Me

Trips to Williamsburg and its magnificent Governor's Mansion were enjoyed by both men but for different reasons. For George Washington the elaborate dinners and balls were the social events of the season. For Will the large enslaved community living in the city offered him many things such as contact with old friends and stories about their ancestral homeland.

acres of land. I was not all work, though. We spent hour after hour at Colonel Washington's favorite pastime, fox hunting. He was known as the finest horseman of his age, and I was required to somehow stay right by his side. In time, I, too, earned a reputation as a fine horseman.

I quickly became a trusted servant and had more freedom than anyone else who served at Mount Vernon. My frequent trips to pick up the mail in Alexandria enabled me to spend time away from the plantation. Colonel Washington also had me accompany him on many trips to Williamsburg, the colonial capital of Virginia, to attend the general assembly. I got to see the Capitol building, the governor's mansion, and even the evening balls. Colonel Washington was on the floor dancing the first dance as well as the last. Our visits to Williamsburg also afforded me the opportunity to spend time with fellow slaves, trading information about relatives and stories about our African homeland, as well as catching up on the political news that might affect our lives.

By then it was the early 1770s and the world as we knew it was beginning to change!

Chapter II

In early 1774 we journeyed to Philadelphia, where Colonel Washington attended the First Continental Congress as one of several delegates from Virginia. The relationship between England and its colonial subjects was strained by then and did not seem to be improving. Well, it was not long before the dark clouds that had been gathering finally erupted into a terrible storm. In April of 1775 the first blood of the American Revolution was shed at the small Massachusetts towns of Lexington and Concord. Two months later the delegates who assembled at the Second Continental Congress selected Virginia delegate Colonel George Washington to lead a new army against Great Britain's troops then headquartered in Boston. Colonel Washington was now appointed General Washington, and I was in for the experience of a lifetime!

I recall the anguish in General Washington's eyes as we returned to our Philadelphia lodgings on the night of June 15, 1775. That was the day that he became commander and needed to inform Mrs. Washington of the plight in which we found ourselves. As we sat by candlelight, General Washington wrote a letter to Mrs. Washington, beginning, "My Dearest, I am now set down to write you on a subject which fills me with inexpressible concern and this concern is greatly aggravated and increased when I reflect on the uneasiness I know it will give you—It has been determined in Congress. . . ." He went on to inform her that he and I would soon be leaving Philadelphia to make our way to Cambridge, Massachusetts, where he would do his best to mold together a fighting force from the "rabble" he had inherited. One can only guess how Mrs. Washington felt as she read those words. As the general wrote on about his own shortcomings in leadership, I was filled with anxiety about the danger that lay ahead for us. I feared being captured and tried as a rebel, exposure to

British army pay voucher prominently signed by King George III, ironically, on George Washington's birthday in the pivotal year of 1776.

smallpox, the destruction of cities around us, and death.

There was no time to worry as, within a few days, we left Philadelphia. For the next eight years General Washington and his fledgling army fought the largest and most experienced army in the world in what we now call the Revolutionary War. A revolution is when a government has its own people rebel against it and its policies. At stake was independence from England and freedom for the inhabitants of the thirteen colonies. But would it bring freedom for slaves too?

The busy hours and days ahead were ones of preparation for our trip and new lives in "camp." The folks we called family were back at Mount Vernon, but now as the general's stature grew, so grew his military family. It had been just the two of us up to this point, and now with secretaries, cooks, and bodyguards we had to learn to live in crowded places with lots of noise and people coming and going continuously. I assumed greater responsibilities; I was entrusted with caring for all of the general's correspondence from the simple to the secret. On the battlefield I carried his field glass that he used to observe troops at a distance. In most cases in the heat of battle I was usually no more than an arm's length away from the general. Well, things were not all bad. The general and I got a taste of home when Mrs. Washington and her

Will quickly became a trusted aide during the Revolutionary War–from carrying General Washington's telescope in battle to keeping safe his most sensitive correspondence. Their years together at war would solidify their relationship.

entourage would arrive in camp for an extended visit. It usually came in the winter months when the fighting subsided and we went into winter quarters. Her visits did wonders for the general's countenance. Making the trip with Mrs. Washington were always a few of the slaves from back at Mount Vernon so for me it was time to catch up on news from home. I was always anxious to hear news of my brother and was overjoyed when informed that he was well. We were sad to see them leave but knew they would be conveying our well being back to those that we loved and missed dearly. By war's end Mrs. Washington would spend at least half of that time with us in camp!

The year 1776 was a momentous one in our young nation's history. For the first fifteen months of the war, we were British subjects fighting our own government. For centuries in the British Isles lords would fight kings, peasants would fight lords and so on until the fighting ended with the winner in charge. That was about to change. In June there were rumors coming from Congress that the British subjects in North America would be declaring the thirteen colonies free and independent states. As much as those in the colonies wanted freedom from King George III and his parliament, they were not seeking freedom for all. The slaves would continue to be the property of the people in the colonies. On July 9th the general received important correspondence from the president of Congress, Mr. Hancock. Washington and I stood in his office as he opened the envelope. He only read for a second or two before he took a seat. As I looked over his shoulder we both read Mr. Jefferson's eloquent and momentous words to ourselves, "When in the course of human events. . . ." The Congress back in Philadelphia had done it! The delegates assembled had declared independence from King George III and his overreaching British government. General Washington knew all too well that putting it on parchment was one thing, but that fighting for it would be a daunting task. The days and months ahead would be the most trying of our lives. Freezing winters, starving troops, ferocious battles, and the cries of the wounded and dying became seared in our memories. "Divine Providence," as the general had often referred it, carried us through those long eight years.

Mr. Jefferson's words also gave me hope, though it turned out to be false hope. I

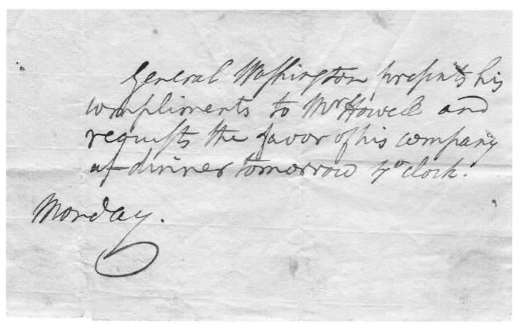

Dinner invitation to congressman David Howell of Rhode Island in the hand of wartime aide Samuel Shaw.

continued to read the Declaration and found phrases such as "all men are created equal" and that God had endowed in all of us certain natural rights such as "life, liberty and the pursuit of happiness." How could men of such distinction, men of such achievement seek their own freedom all the while owning other human beings? With the realities of war upon us all, I did not have time to pursue answers to my question.

The year 1776 ended with a brilliant and inspirational military stroke on my master's behalf. From Pennsylvania he reinvigorated the last few thousand troops under his command for a trip across an ice-choked river. The name of the river was the Delaware. General Washington chose Christmas night to lead an attack on the Hessian garrison at Trent's Town, New Jersey. Hessians were German soldiers who

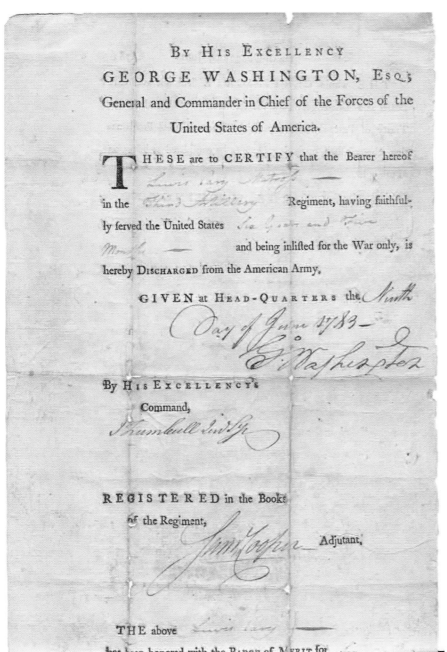

By His Excellency
GEORGE WASHINGTON, Esq;
General and Commander in Chief of the Forces of the
United States of America.

THESE are to CERTIFY that the Bearer hereof _Lewis Cary Matross_ in the _Third Artillery_ Regiment, having faithfully served the United States _Six Years and Five Months_ and being inlisted for the War only, is hereby DISCHARGED from the American Army.

GIVEN at HEAD-QUARTERS the _Ninth Day of June 1783—_

G Washington

By His Excellency's
Command,
Trumbull Sec'y

REGISTERED in the Books
of the Regiment,
_____ Adjutant.

THE above _Lewis Cary_
has been honored with the Badge of Merit for . . .

Revolutionary War discharge of Lewis Cary who served as a matross in the Third Artillery Regiment. It was signed by George Washington in 1783 as the Commander in Chief of the Continental Army.

were hired by the British government to fight alongside British soldiers. To top it off, there was a blinding snowstorm that night. The attack was successful, and the small town of Trent's Town resounded in the ears of patriots for many years to come. Our confidence grew from that day on. Despite freezing winter encampments at Jockey Hollow and the Valley Forge, we fought to a draw or drove the enemy from the field in places called Prince Town, Monmouth Court House and Cowpens. The fighting spanned from as far north as Canada all the way south to Georgia!

The final battle of the war took us back to our home state of Virginia, where there was a tiny village just south of Williamsburg. With the help of the French army and navy, commanded by General Rochambeau and Admiral de Grasse, General Washington trapped British General Cornwallis in the village of York Town. After a long and terrible siege with no possibility for escape, Lord Cornwallis made the decision to surrender. As Cornwallis and Washington discussed terms word began to spread throughout the thirteen colonies that the end was drawing near. Yes, the world had truly been turned upside down!

On September 3, 1783, the Revolutionary War officially ended. In France, the Treaty of Paris was signed, declaring the American colonies free and independent states. General Washington did not go down in history as the greatest military tactician in the world, but rather he is remembered for his strong character. He had courage and determination in the face of great odds and his desire to leave fame behind for the simple life of a farmer would mark him for even greater deeds.

While there were free black men who served in the war, many of my fellow enslaved African brothers also served bravely in the war, and some had died for the cause of independence. Despite our cooperation and loyalty, we were still considered the property of our masters. Many would fight in place of their masters with the promise of freedom. At wars end some received it, some did not. They were well trained and disciplined and I know they greatly impressed General Washington as they fought bravely alongside their white brethren-in-arms. There were those observers who thought that as much as twenty percent of the entire army could have been comprised of black soldiers. At wars end the colonies were free from British rule, but for many of us who lived in bondage freedom remained a dream.

Christmas Eve of 1783, General Washington and I turned our horses toward the large, white candle-lit mansion with the smoke billowing from its chimneys off in the distance. After eight long years, we returned home to family and friends at Mount Vernon. I continued in my duties as the general's most trusted servant. Although it was never openly discussed, after our years at war together there was a new bond between us, a kinship that he shared with no one else but me at Mount Vernon.

In the weeks and months that followed, I preformed my duties about the mansion wondering, would freedom be in my future for my devoted service during the war? Upon my arrival home I had learned of a Virginian law passed in 1782 that now allowed a master to free a slave without the permission of the state, which had been the case prior. Could this be what I have been waiting for? Well, two new additions to the family were just what I needed to take my mind away from this nagging question. While away at war my brother Frank and his wife Lucy became the parents of two boys. When we arrived home little Mike was just an infant but Edmund was already three years old! It was a joy to have the second generation of Lees at Mount Vernon.

Known then as the Pennsylvania State House, Independence Hall played an important role in the formation of the new nation. It was here that George Washington was selected to command the Continental Army, the Declaration of Independence was signed, and the Constitutional Convention met with George Washington as president. Will would have known the building well.

Chapter III

The mid-1780s brought talk of the creation of a new type of government that the world had never seen. Quite possibly this would be the event we servants had been waiting and hoping for.

General Washington was the beacon of light once more as some of the greatest minds on the continent gathered again in Philadelphia for the Constitutional Convention in 1787 to discuss and formulate "a more perfect union." Certainly the topic of slavery would be part of the proceedings, I thought. After proving our dedication during the war, freedom would surely be around the corner.

General Washington served as the convention president and worked diligently for

Colonel Washington and Me

its ratification using his universal stature from the war years. Once again I was privy to a bird's-eye view of the proceedings. Just think, I was there when our government was created! I got to see some of the fruits of our labor from those long days assisting General Washington during the Revolutionary War. But what about slavery? Were we to be disappointed again? My worst fears were realized as the convention came and went with the existence of slavery still in tact.

As I was fortunate to read and write and was always at General Washington's side, I was more keenly aware of his sentiments on the topic of slavery. He mandated that his slave families should no longer be separated. Those of the general's "people" who were no longer physically able to work were to remain under his care for the duration of their lives and medical treatment came quickly when needed. White overseers received sharp reprimands for inappropriate treatment of slaves. Still I wondered, why not free all of us now? Even the man he was closest to, the Marquis de Lafayette, begged him to put the finishing touch on his reputation as the father of all liberty and free his slaves. I had witnessed him on so many occasions act swiftly and decisively,

After leg injuries no longer allowed him to serve as George Washington's valet, Will took up the shoemaking trade on the estate. The day was not complete without a visit from the general.

and yet on this topic he was seemingly powerless.

Although I struggled emotionally with the question of freedom at least I was healthy. In the mid to late 1780s that changed. Two separate accidents, one while surveying in 1785 and the other on an icy day in Alexandria in 1788, rendered both of my legs almost completely useless. I realized quickly that I would no longer be able to serve in the only job I had known since coming to Mount Vernon. The physical and emotional strain was almost too much to bear, and I knew I had to do something. Rather than dwell on my shortcomings, I consulted with General Washington. He recommended that I try something where I could sit and at the same time would be making a useful contribution to the Mount Vernon community. He mentioned that there was almost always a shortage of footwear for the many folks that resided on the estate. Well, I quickly picked up the shoemaker trade and have been doing it ever since. It did allow me to contribute in some way without having to be on my feet. Living in a house near the mansion resulted in frequent visits from General Washington that brightened my days. Our relationship of many years continued to grow as we both moved along in age.

One day an old friend from General Washington's days in Congress came to visit him and our lives changed again! It was the 14th of April when a carriage arrived. As Charles Thomson stepped from that carriage the general knew he was back to a life of public service. The federal Congress had directed Mr. Thomson, a long-time secretary of Congress, to visit the person elected the first president of the United States and inform him of his election. After a brief, friendly exchange, Mr. Thomson then made the news official with a message from the president of the Senate. From an adjacent room I heard Mr. Thomson finish, "and be considered as a sure pledge of the affection

Excitement filled the air as George Washington, along with family and friends, prepared to leave Mount Vernon for New York City, the first capital of the new government. Here he would be inaugurated as the very first president of the United States.

and support you are to expect from a free and enlightened people." The very people that he helped to free had elected him president!

It occurred to me that ultimately the entire family and staff would soon be leaving for New York, the site of the new federal capital, and leaving me behind! I quickly appealed to my old friend for permission to make the trip. With Washington's permission, I immediately packed my finest clothing.

We only had a day or two to prepare General Washington and his staff for their move to New York, where he would be inaugurated. An air of excitement greeted the morning of April 16th as the presidential entourage was about to leave Mount Vernon for the long trip north. Although it was a joyous time I sensed an air of foreboding in General Washington. He entrusted his deepest thoughts to no one but his diary that day as he wrote, "About ten o'clock I bade adieu to Mount Vernon and to private life, and to domestic felicity; and with a mind oppressed with more anxious and painful sensations than I have words to express, set out for New York. . . ."

The soon-to-be president and his staff were finally on the road north. On our way to New York, we passed through the many cities and towns that were so pivotal in our days fighting the Revolutionary War. Emotions ran high as General Washington made his way through Philadelphia and crossed the Delaware River at Trent's Town. The future president and those traveling with him were overwhelmed by the reception received at the entrance to every town and every bridge crossed. Gun salutes, candle-lit dinners, and elaborate balls awaited us in every town and city!

Mrs. Washington and two of her four grandchildren, Nelly Custis and George Washington Parke Custis, would not leave the estate for New York until a month later, arriving in New York on May 28th. The soon-to-be-first lady was in the capable hands of Robert Lewis, the general's nephew from Fredericksburg, Virginia. Mrs. Washington and party received virtually the same reception at every stop as the general did on his trip north!

Unfortunately my trip was cut short. It seems that my weary old legs did not take well to all of the traveling. I got as far as Philadelphia when it was determined that I should stay behind to seek medical attention. Soon-to-be President Washington attempted to persuade me to make my way back to Mount Vernon, but I would have none of it. I was determined to make my way to New York and be of service to him. My time in Philadelphia was longer than I expected even though I was treated by the best doctors that the city had to offer. As my health deteriorated so did my hope of being witness to the inauguration of the first president. I ended up having to read about it in the newspapers. It must have been a splendid event. Gunboats roared as the presidential barge neared the city and it was rumored that porpoises swam alongside as if they knew America's first president was onboard the boat! The parade after the ceremony rivaled any that North America had ever seen.

Reading the events in the newspaper made me even more determined to get better quickly so I could join the Washington's in New York. The president's secretary, Tobias Lear, wrote to the man taking care of me, "he has been an old and faithful servant. This is enough for the President to gratify him in every reasonable wish." Just what I had been waiting for! Soon Mr. Lear made arrangements for my trip from Philadelphia to New York. It was Wednesday, June 17th, two months after leaving Mount Vernon, when I arrived at the new capital and the presidential household.

The presidential mansion, as one could imagine, was a beehive of activity. It reminded both of us of our days at headquarters during the Revolutionary War. The president's home was also his office so it was a mixture of business and entertainment. I knew upon my arrival that I would be in no physical condition to assist directly in the management of the home, but I could lend my many years of expertise to those who could do the job. The president and Mrs. Washington relied on their most trusted and capable servants to manage affairs. Those who traveled from Mount Vernon did their best to have the Washingtons feel as much at home as possible, from Hercules the cook to Oney, Mrs. Washington's personal maid.

For many guests who visited, being served by the president's slaves was a perplexing fact indeed. It was troubling to citizens from states or foreign countries, where the practice of slavery had been outlawed, to be waited on by enslaved individuals. This was supposed to be the capital of freedom.

I had spent my adult years hoping that the momentous events that we had both been a part of—the War of Independence, the writing of the Constitution, his ascension to the presidency— would in some way reshape Washington's attitudes toward slavery. After witnessing his many slaves working harder than ever in the new capital I had made up my mind that I was disappointed for the last time. I forced myself to not dwell on the negatives, and instead I tried to look at his many accomplishments for mankind. At this point I could only hope that future generations would have the courage and strength to end slavery at long last.

Washington's years as president were not easy. Many who fought in the war and helped to establish the new government now began to have differences of opinion on what shape and direction the new republic should take. It was difficult for me to read newspapers that criticized the president after all he had sacrificed for his country. He continued to treat friends and adversaries with the same respect and fairness that had

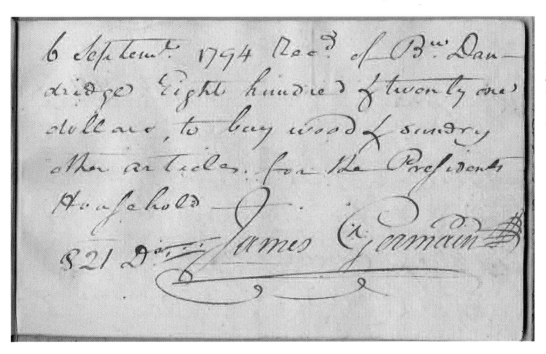

Receipt from the presidential mansion for "wood and sundry other articles for the Presidents household" when the capital was in Philadelphia.
Dated September of 1794.

become his hallmark.

At the close of our first year in New York it was decided that the government would be moved a bit further south to accommodate those traveling from southern states. So the president packed up again and moved to Philadelphia, the city that meant so much to both of us. President Washington would spend the next three years here to complete his term. By this time I was back at Mount Vernon for good. He must have been envious for he missed his home dearly during his time as president

although he would occasionally make it back for a couple of weeks of relaxation. Those close to him had hoped that these would be his final years in public service, as one could see the stress of the job beginning to take its toll on him. Washington himself had expressed on many occasions his desire to retire at the end of the first term and return to his beloved farm. Fellow Virginian Thomas Jefferson pleaded with him, though, to consider a second term so that the new government would not collapse. With great reluctance he agreed to be considered by the Electoral College for another term of four years.

The world of politics and pressures from other nations made the last four years of his public service probably the most difficult. Some good came of it as the government decided once again to move the capital. The planned city would be in the image and likeness of the new republic. A president's mansion and wide streets with great views were just a sampling of what was to come. The idea began to develop in the early 1790s with the government moving there for the beginning of the new millennium. The new site would be close to Mount Vernon, just on the other side of the Potomack River, between two existing towns with which we were very familiar, George Town and Alexandria. George Town was the namesake of King George the II. Now it would be rivaled by the name of another great man; the new capital would be called Washington! What a thrill it was for those of us who had been with him from the beginning to know that his name would be associated with one of the great cities of the world. During and after his term in office he would make frequent trips to check on the city's development. Although he never lived in Washington, D.C., General Washington played an enormous role in how the city and its buildings would appear, from selecting the sight for the president's mansion to laying the cornerstone for the capital.

Well, after many long and trying days, the time we had all been looking forward to was finally upon us—the president's retirement to Mount Vernon. The world was also

Shortly after his retirement from the presidency in 1797, it was back to business as evidenced by Washington's handwritten and signed receipt for rent received on his land in three different Virginian counties.

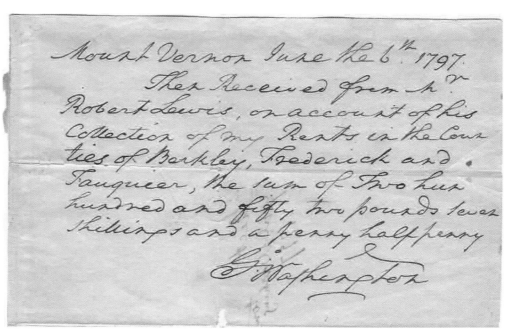

watching and waiting for a slightly different reason. In March of 1797 nations far and wide waited to see if this American experiment in government would work. Would the transfer of power be successful? John Adams of Massachusetts had been elected president, and it was now time for George Washington to give back his authority. Would he continue to rule indefinitely as so many kings and queens had done, or

would he abide by the Constitution and see Mr. Adams inaugurated? On a cold March morning, Washington walked by himself from the president's mansion to the House of Representatives chamber to witness the ceremony. He stood quietly and erectly, dressed in what was described as a black suit and powdered hair, as he heard Mr. Adams repeat the oath of office.

Chapter IV

With the exception of being called upon by President Adams to assemble an army for a possible war with France that never materialized his retirement to Mount Vernon was complete. I was still at my residence close to the Mount Vernon mansion, where my work as a shoemaker continued in earnest. My physical disability no longer allowed me the opportunity to join former President Washington on his daily ride to inspect his five farms, but when he returned for his three o'clock dinner he always made a point to stop by to bid good day and or to see if there was something he could do for me.

In his letter of April 24th, 1799 Baltimore resident John Campbell White describes to a friend his visit to Mount Vernon just four days prior; "on Sunday evening I returned from Mount Vernon wither a small party of us had gone on a visit to General Washington, we were received with much politeness & civility, had the honour of dining with the General & were strongly pressed to stay all night."

After his many years in public service there was much that needed to be done on the property, and he wasted little time getting to work. Mount Vernon was busy once again, and the carpenters, painters, and blacksmith worked constantly to keep up. Busy also were the house and kitchen staff as old friends and complete strangers would visit and stay for days and sometimes weeks at a time. General and Mrs. Washington knew that with fame also came great responsibility. Old comrades in arms—the many officers and men with whom we lived and fought alongside during those hard eight years that now seemed so long ago—made frequent stops. There existed a special bond between all who had fought in the war, and that bond seemed to grow stronger as the years progressed. While visiting with General Washington, these special guests would inquire about my well being. The general would explain that with the exception of two bad legs I enjoyed relatively good health. Whenever he would mention that I enjoyed visits from our old brethren, they would call upon me at my quarters. Our reunions were emotional ones, as we recalled our previous hardships and glory.

Life went on as normal at Mount Vernon. On February 22, 1799, we celebrated not only General Washington's birthday, but also the wedding of Miss Nelly Custis, Mrs. Washington's granddaughter. Since her father was deceased she selected her dear step-grandfather to escort her down the main staircase at the mansion house. It was just about dusk as General Washington and Nellie appeared at the top of the stairs. The bride looked beautiful and General Washington equally as handsome as he wore his old continental colors of blue and buff. We felt like family as the slaves about the mansion were not only invited to the ceremony but also invited to partake in the wedding feast that followed.

The century was closing rapidly and would, no doubt, have us reflecting on past accomplishments as well as looking toward the future. What an exciting future it promised to be. All within the Mount Vernon family were anxiously awaiting the federal government moving to the District of Columbia and the city of Washington. Congress would occupy the new Capitol building and the United States' chief executive would inhabit the new presidential mansion. With certainty General Washington would be in attendance at all of the festivities. He was still very popular and found himself the guest of honor at a July 4th celebration in Alexandria, the last one in the century.

Mount Vernon continued to be a favorite destination for many people, the general referring to his home as "a well resorted tavern." He also made certain there was time for family. After guests retired, he and Mrs. Washington would sit quietly. He would look through the day's newspaper and read aloud when he found something he thought was humorous. After Washington's two terms as president, the first family welcomed their lack of civic responsibility.

During Washington's many visits to my quarters I began to sense a change in his behavior and attitudes. He talked more of his increased age, especially after a prolonged illness of Mrs. Washington's and the passing of the last of his brothers. He was also more actively engaged in attempting to rent some of his farms plus the gristmill and distillery. A severe drought that resulted in crop loss the summer of 1799 further distressed him. He more frequently spoke about the many slave families that were his responsibility and what their futures may be. The general had referred to "his people" many times in the past to me, but now there seemed to be a look of uncertainty on his face and a certain unsettled tone in his voice. I also got word from several of the servants who worked in the mansion that the general's behavior had

changed. He spent long hours late at night working in his study. He wrote for hours on end without interruption. At about the same time he made a detailed list of the slaves that he owned as well as those who were under his guidance but belonged to Mrs. Washington. Listed were names, ages, occupations, spouses and children. It seemed as though he was preparing for the future even as he continued to enjoy near-perfect health.

Summer turned to fall and with it came much welcome cooler days. Harvest time was busy, but everyone knew that shortly there would be much less work as the sun set earlier. General Washington continued to be extremely active with trips to inspect the progress at the new capital city. In November the weather was pleasant enough for him to survey one of his many properties and that of a neighbor.

My favorite time of the year was approaching swiftly. With a winter's worth of firewood stacked and a couple of light snowfalls already, the Christmas season was surely not far off. For many years Virginia has been known for its festive celebrations at the coming holiday. There was much excitement, with the kitchen and its bake oven working overtime. I found nothing more pleasing than to look out of my window and see the candlelit mansion with smoke billowing out of its chimneys and to hear in the distance Miss Nelly playing old English carols on her harpsichord as family and

In the solitude of his candle lit study, George Washington wrote his last will and testament. From that twenty-eight page document came one of his most enduring legacies—the freedom of his slaves.

The President's Mansion was almost entirely George Washington's idea–from selecting the site to overseeing the building's construction. Here Will rides along on one of the General's frequent inspections. We know the building today as the White House.

visiting friends sung along. For the servant staff, it was many additional hours of work, but our faith carried us through. The Christmas season reminded us of the promise of a new life. If we were not to find freedom in this life, surely we would find it in the next!

Chapter V

December 13, 1799, was a beautiful day with about three inches of snow in the morning. The mansion was the center of a small village of buildings that were cozy with the quiet hush that the snow brought. The afternoon became perfectly clear and the general took advantage of the opportunity to make his way to the front lawn and mark a couple of trees that he desired to be cut. With the exception of that and penning a note to one of his farm managers, he relaxed most of the day, which was unusual for him. The day prior he had gone for his daily ride. There had been light snow at the start of his ride, but it had turned to hail and then a cold rain. As a result he awoke on the thirteenth with a scratchy throat and deemed it best to remain "at home all day."

The events of the next twenty-four hours would bring news that would shock the world and change our lives forever. At about three in the morning on December 14, the general woke with his sore throat having gotten considerably worse. Alarmed, Mrs. Washington was about to summon help, but General Washington persuaded her to remain in bed, fearing for her health should she be exposed to the cold morning air. Ultimately her maid Caroline arrived to stir up the fire and Mrs. Washington sent her to summon Mr. Lear, the general's long-time secretary, to Washington's bedchamber. Mr. Lear understood that medical attention was needed, and he sent out notices to several doctors who made their way to Mount Vernon throughout the course of the day to attend to the ailing hero. Among those doctors was James Craik, the general's good friend from the old French and Indian War days. Washington's situation steadily grew worse. With his usual dignity, he resigned himself to the fact that this day would

be his last. Mrs. Washington never left his side. Also in attendance were two maids, Caroline, Moll, and my nephew Christopher who only left the room to bring back various remedies requested by the doctors. I was also told that Mr. Lear served him faithfully in his final hours, granting his every request.

As day turned to night and with the situation at its gravest, the general gave his final commands. He instructed Mrs. Washington as to which of two wills was to be used. He was to be "decently" placed in the old family tomb, but only after he was gone for three days. Mr. Lear silently acknowledged these requests. Saturday, December 14, 1799, George Washington took his last breath. One of the physicians that attended him later noted that the general "retained the full possession of his intellect, when he expired without a struggle." The old commander was in control right to the end!

Expressions of grief resounded throughout the country. It would take a week or two for the news to reach Europe. All eyes turned to Mount Vernon as the estate prepared for the general's funeral. Just several days after his passing I was able to witness George Washington's coffin being removed from the large dining room and, in a procession befitting his stature, make its way to the old family tomb overlooking the river. There, on December 18, a simple service was held, accompanied by the boom of artillery.

As I bid farewell to my old friend, our previous lives together ran through my mind like the acts of a stage play. I saw two young men fox hunting. I recalled visiting the Virginian capital of Williamsburg with its splendid governor's mansion, as well as many trips to the city of Philadelphia. I remembered crossing the ice-choked Delaware River on a snowy Christmas night, and the surrender of the British army at York Town. My mind then turned to the rewards for all of our hard work and sacrifice: the formation of the new government, the general becoming president, and finally our retirement to the place we both loved and called home.

While pondering how my life would change now that the general was gone, the Christmas season came and went, failing to lift my spirits. The mansion and its environs continued to be a melancholy place as all of us who resided there did our best to get used to life without the man who meant so much to us all. We marked with sadness the coming and going of the new year and the new century, an event he had looked forward to seeing so much.

Mrs. Washington was kept busy with her grandchildren and their families, some of whom lived here, and those who made frequent visits. In addition there were the many legal matters that needed to be addressed as a result of the general's passing. The executors of his estate made numerous visits to comb over the many directives he had left in his twenty-eight page will and to do an inventory of every room in the mansion and every building on the property. The document began with the requisite mention of Mrs. Washington and what she would naturally retain as his wife. Thousands of acres were divided among relatives, his five swords were given to nephews, stock in various business ventures benefited educational institutions, and so on.

Rumors of something momentous in the general's will were circulating. What could he possibly achieve in death that would be greater than any of his many accomplishments during life?

The news hit Mount Vernon, the nation, and the world like a lightning bolt. He had done it! I could scarcely believe what I was hearing. On January 10, 1800, the news that no one had expected spread rapidly. In his will, Washington wrote, "upon the decease of my wife, it is my will and desire that all the slaves whom I hold in my own right shall receive their freedom." Earth shattering! He had answered his friend

Lafayette's call to solidify his reputation as the father of freedom. The final chapter of his life would be his greatest. The general went on to spell out the details once we were free. His executors were to see that his instructions were "religiously fulfilled" as it related to education, pensions, food, clothing, and living quarters. We would be compensated for life for the service we had given him!

Lightning struck again in the form of a gentle knock on the door of my quarters. The messenger delivered news that I could hardly comprehend. I read it once, twice, a third time. My mind had difficulty processing the words my eyes were reading; "and to my mulatto man William (calling himself William Lee) I give immediate freedom." Immediate freedom! He continued, "& this I give him as a testimony of my sense of

For Will, freedom has come at a high price—the loss of his good friend. George Washington's wish when he passed away was to be placed in the old family tomb. In the early 1830s his coffin was moved to its current resting place on the Mount Vernon grounds. The old tomb is preserved and can be seen today at Mount Vernon.

his attachment to me, and for his faithful service during the Revolutionary War."

And so that is our story. In addition to my freedom I received food, clothing, and an annual pension for the rest of my life. The general knew Mount Vernon was my home for the past thirty-one years, so I was also granted the option of living out my days on the estate. It was an easy decision to stay and I continued to dabble in the shoemaking trade here on the property. As time went on and most of the Washington family eventually passed away or moved from here, I became an important link to the

past for the many guests that continued to visit the home of our hero. It was particularly thrilling to have Mr. Peale, the man who had painted General Washington's portrait so many times, come to Mount Vernon to see me.

I do regret as I finish my story that slavery does still exist here in our country and the general's legacy of freeing his people will not be complete until all slaves are free. All I can do is hope and pray that it will end soon. I will not rest, and if I am gone before it ends my soul will not be at peace until this dreaded curse of slavery is eradicated from this country and around the world. My other regret as I finish my story is that I never had the opportunity to thank him for the freedom he knew I should have had all along. It took me many years to realize we both struggled for freedom. Mine was apparent. His struggle was to unchain himself from the moral burden of slave ownership that had haunted him since age eleven. Was he a perfect man? He would be the first to tell you no. Was he a great man? I will be the first to tell you yes! Now, my young friends, you know the story of Colonel Washington and me.

Epilogue

Little or nothing is known about the lives of individual slaves during the eighteenth century. There are several exceptions, and Will Lee is one of them. Most, if not all, that we know about Will is as a result of his close association with George Washington. We can trace the development of their relationship through letters and diary entries that George Washington kept so meticulously throughout the course of his life. Others associated with the Washingtons and life at Mount Vernon have contributed as well. One of the most telling is the recollections of Martha Washington's grandson, George Washington Parke Custis. Raised at Mount Vernon by George and Martha Washington, his words are an interesting insight into life with the Washingtons. One's speculation that a close relationship had developed between Washington and Lee becomes reality when we read the second "item" in George Washington's will, where William Lee is granted his freedom.

When Will arrives at Mount Vernon as a young man he is known as "Billy." Over time he becomes "William" to General Washington. Could this be a tiny window into the maturing of George Washington's changing attitude toward slavery that would ultimately culminate in the freeing of his "people"?

In a letter dated August 17, 1799, to his nephew Robert Lewis, it is glaringly apparent that years of slave ownership became a financial and moral burden for George Washington. In that letter he strongly reiterates his opposition to the sale of any of his slaves and the separation of families. On or around the 9th of July, while he was still in perfect health and looking to cross the threshold into the next century, Washington set the example for America when he granted freedom to his slaves in his will.

William Lee did in fact live out his days as a free man at Mount Vernon. Oral tradition says that he is buried in an unmarked grave in the "slave burial ground" not far from where his old friend Washington was laid to rest. George Washington predicated the freedom of the rest of his slaves on the passing of Mrs. Washington. She, however, elected to grant them their freedom in 1801, the year before her death. Washington was, in fact, the only one of the four early Virginian presidents (Jefferson, Madison and, Monroe) to free all of his slaves.

William's prayers for slavery to finally end would not be answered until many years after he had passed on from this life. In 1863, at about the half way point of the American Civil War, President Abraham Lincoln signed the Emancipation

Proclamation. It outlawed slavery but only in the states that had seceded from the unic during the war. In 1865 the thirteenth amendment to the Constitution, the very Constitution to which Will Lee was an eyewitness to its creation, would finally outlaw slavery in the United States.

There are differing references to the year of Will's passing. The first is a ledger entry Lawrence Lewis, George Washington's nephew, that places his death around the end of 1810 or early 1811. The later reference by historian Benson J. Lossing has Will passing about 1828, "at a very advanced age." If this second reference is accurate, Will's age at time of his death would have been around seventy-six—quite an old age for someone in the early nineteenth century. Lewis, as one of the general's executors was the individua that ensured that William was cared for per the general's instructions. It is likely that h dates on William's passing are accurate.

At the close of the Revolutionary War, George Washington had his officers gathere Fraunces Tavern in New York City for what would be their final dinner together. As th dinner began to wind down, Washington addressed the men who had stuck with him during the darkest days of the war. In a tearful farewell he uttered these final words, "I r devoutly wish that your latter days may be as prosperous and happy as your former ones have been glorious and honorable."

For him and Will, I think they were!

Ashworth, M. W., and J. A. Carroll. *George Washington: A Biography.* Vol. 7. New York: Charles Scribner's Sons, 1957.

Flexner, James Thomas. *George Washington.* 4 vols. Boston and Toronto: Little, Brown and Company, 1969.

Freeman, Douglas Southall. *George Washington: A Biography.* 6 vols. New York: Charles Scribner's Sons, 1948–57. E

Thompson, Mary. E-mail message to author. February 2, 2011.

————. E-mail message to author. October 14, 2011.

————. E-mail message to author. November 21, 2011.

Washington, George. *The Diaries of George Washington.* 6 vols. Edited by Donald Jackson and Dorothy Twohig. Charlottesville and London: University of Virginia Press, 1976.

————. *The Last Will and Testament of George Washington.* Edited by Dr. John C. Fitzpatrick. Virginia: The Mount Vernon Ladies' Association of the Union, 1939.

————. *The Papers of George Washington: Retirement Series.* 4 vols. Edited by Dorothy Twohig, Philander D. Chase, and Beverly H. Runge. Charlottesville and London: University Press of Virginia, 1999.

————. *The Papers of George Washington: Revolutionary War Series.* 12 vols. Edited by W. W. Abbot, Dorothy Twohig, and Philander D. Chase. Charlottesville: University Press of Virginia, 1985.